Welcome to the Million Dollar Body™ Club!

Congratulations on joining this unprecedented wellness revolution created and supported by a community of people just like you, dedicated to improving their lives! This book—exclusively from Million Dollar Body™—will help you make smart eating decisions and enhance your results!

As a Club member, you have access to the ultimate support and motivation you need to succeed, including:

- Your personalized meal plan and shopping list
- VIP access and advice from celebrity experts
- 10% savings on our nutrition and fitness products
- Easy interactive tools for tracking your progress
- A unique opportunity to become a Success Story and WIN up to $250,000!

Go to MillionDollarBody.com and follow the 3 easy steps below to access your VIP benefits...

MDB MILLION DOLLAR BODY™

1. **Enter your email address.**
Make sure to use the same email address you used when you joined the Club.

2. **Enter your temporary password:** WELLNESS
You only need your temporary password for your first login.

3. **Create your new password.**

Log in to MillionDollarBody.com daily!

Start your transformation right away! Log in now!

Visit MillionDollarBody.com Today!

Super Fuel:

The easy way to melt off pounds

Fat Burners

We have to eat in order to lose weight. This simple truth always elicits a certain amount of skepticism. It's deeply engraved in our minds that we must avoid calories, refuse fatty foods, and banish evil carbohydrates! And it's because so many of us believe this that so many people in this country are overweight. But whether we follow the latest diet in Hollywood or the one practiced at the office, nothing works in the long run. The bitter result is the "yo-yo effect." We've struggled tediously to starve off those last few pounds and have finally arrived at our ideal weight when suddenly the yo-yo hits the end of its string and jumps back up to the top, each time climbing a little higher. Sound familiar?

It's time to put a stop to it all! Change your life. Throw out all calorie-saving measures. You have to eat to lose weight. And in the future you'll notice that when you fill up your tank with "super," you will feel more energetic, alive, and joyful than you ever dreamed possible. The following five principles will guide you on your journey:

1. Carbohydrates with a low-glycemic index let you drop pounds
2. Fat doesn't just turn to fat—you need some fat in your diet

3. Protein melts away the body's extra padding
4. Without vital nutrients, our metabolism grinds to a halt
5. Without exercise, we can't even begin

METABOLISM—THE WHEEL OF LIFE

Your body contains a natural wonder, your metabolism. Think of it as the wheel of life, or a complicated biological system that converts the food you eat to energy, body tissues, creative thoughts, and joyful feelings. You determine all that you are, the way you feel, and the amount of strength and joy you experience each day by what you choose to eat. The only thing is, your system is millions of years old. Four million years ago, our first human ancestor's biological system was programmed to run on a naturally pure diet of lean meat, fruits, roots, vegetables, and grains. Our system has remained the same but the fuel has changed dramatically. Up to 75% of what we eat is a product of industry. Admittedly, these days no one wants to sit in the kitchen, plucking a chicken. Being able to take our vegetables from the freezer saves us time and encourages good health. At the same time, however, we overload our bodies with substances that our genes don't recognize. There's no genetic program for metabolizing instant soups, ketchup, candy bars, and the like. The body strives in vain to defend itself, contracting illnesses of civilization such as obesity, diabetes, gout, heart disease, chronic fatigue, depression, and cancer.

THE WRONG FUEL

If we treated our cars in the same way we treat our bodies, they would never even make it out of the garage. From morning 'till night we fill our tanks with the worst kind of fuel, even though we know this destroys the engine: Fast food and chocolate, white flour and sugar, preservatives and dyes, artificial additives and contaminants—all of them unfamiliar to our metabolism. Larger amounts of these substances throw off the delicate balance of hormones in our bodies. As a result we become fat—and unhappy. But we can take precautionary measures by avoiding processed products. Excessive weight is our body's response to a lack of vital nutrients. Packaged foods often contain a hodgepodge of dead nutrients, supplemented with 7000 flavorings and a few token vitamins to promote sales.

HOW TO LOSE WEIGHT

Give your body's 70 billion cells the vital nutrients, basic materials, and energy they need and they will thank you with a lively dance of hormones, a powerful immune system, firm muscles, nerves of steel, active organs, and an attractive figure. If you neglect even one nutrient, your body will respond with fatigue, bad moods, dull hair, and extra pounds. It is a lack of certain nutrients that makes you fat. It is nutrients that help burn off the fat. Nutrients are the fat burners.

Low-Glycemic

Warning— sugar is stronger than your will!

Carbohydrates

Carbohydrates come from such diverse sources as sugar and honey, chocolate, candy, whole-grain bread, fruits, and vegetables. The difference between them is that some of these foods make us fatter, while others are true fat burners that melt off the pounds. It all depends on their glycemic index.

THE GLYCEMIC INDEX

The glycemic index is your fate. It determines whether you will be fat or thin. The glycemic index formula is simple: Carbohydrates that raise your blood sugar (in other words, those that enter your bloodstream rapidly) have a glycemic index of over 50, meaning that they have the potential to make you fat. These include sugar, sweetened beverages, polished rice, white flour, chips, and many more processed products (see table on page 5). Low-glycemic foods (those with an index of under 50) stabilize your blood sugar level and are genuine fat burners. These include the natural carbohydrates derived from fruits, vegetables, and whole-grain products.

THE POWER OF SUGAR

Whenever you eat, you trigger a dance of hormones in your body. These hormones con-trol your energy metabolism. They either deposit the fat on your hips or take it off and transport it to the mitochondria, tiny kilns in your cells that combust the fat into heat. Glucagon, for example, is a fat-burning hormone. Insulin, on the other hand, is a fat storer. Whenever you eat a high-glycemic food such as candy, white flour, or polished rice, the sugar molecules quickly pass from the intestines to the bloodstream. Your pancreas doesn't have a clue about what is happening, since refined food wasn't introduced until 500 years ago, so it panics. It dispatches an entire armada of insulin to halt the advancing sugar barrage. The insulin either diverts the sugar from the blood stream to the muscles or converts it to fat on your hips. Your blood sugar drops dramatically and rapidly and your brain's sugar supply is depleted. If you have no more sugar in your blood, you lose the ability to concentrate. You become distracted, nervous, and tired. Your brain feels threatened and soon responds with a ravenous craving for something sweet. And you give it what it wants because sugar is stronger than your will. And the problem is, if you start your day with sugar you won't be able to end it with-out sugar.

INSULIN WEIGHT GAIN

Carbohydrate craving is a phenomenon that causes people to gain weight. Usually, quick carbohydrates are combined with fat, whether in chocolate bars or chips. The insulin created by eating these substances sends the fat straight to your fat cells where it gets locked away. As long as insulin dominates your blood, glucagon, the fat-burning hormone, doesn't have a chance. As soon as you change your diet to fat burners, foods with a low-glycemic index, glucagon will take over and send the fat to your muscles to be combusted. As for high-glycemic foods, enjoy them in modera-tion and try not to combine them with fat.

FAT STORERS —
HIGH-GLYCEMIC FOODS

Beverages: Beer 110; soft drinks, colas, sweetened fruit juices 80–100

Sweeteners: Honey 75; sugar 75; chocolate 70; jellies and jams 60

Bread: White sandwich bread 95; pretzels 85; French bread 70; mixed-grain rye bread 65

Potatoes: Fried potatoes 95; mashed potatoes 90; french fries 80; boiled potatoes 65

Fruits and vegetables: Carrots 85; winter squash 75; corn 70; watermelon 70; pineapple 65; raisins 65; bananas 60; honeydew melon 60

Grain products: Cornflakes, popcorn 85; rice cakes, puffed rice 80; sweetened muesli 70; corn chips 75; crackers 75; croissants 70; cornmeal 70; wheat flour 70; instant rice 90; polished white rice 70; couscous 60; pasta 60

FAT BURNERS —
LOW-GLYCEMIC FOODS

Sweeteners: Unsweetened jam 30; fruit-flavored ice cream (unsweetened, homemade) 35; unsweetened chocolate (over 70% cocoa) 20

Bread: Whole-wheat or bran bread 50; pumpernickel 40; whole rye bread 40

Fruits and vegetables: Fresh vegetables 15; mushrooms 15; fresh vegetable juices 15; fresh fruits 10–30; freshly squeezed fruit juices (unsweetened) 40; dried apricots 30; soybeans 15; lentils 30; peas 50

Grain products: Whole-grain unsweetened muesli 40; oatmeal 40; rye 35; whole-grain rice 50; whole-grain pasta 30

Miscellaneous: Whole-milk dairy products approx. 35; low-fat milk 30; plain unsweet-ened yogurt 15; nuts 15–30

Fat Alone

The right fats burn off unwanted padding

is not the Enemy

You need fat to burn fat. Even the most scorned fattener is actually a fat burner. Studies show that athletes who avoid all fat will suddenly gain weight while their muscles shrink. And no wonder! Essential fatty acids are as important as vitamins. Without them, your body is unable to produce fat-burning hormones. Fat isn't just your number one source of energy; it calms your nerves, builds your cells, makes your skin smooth and youthful, and cushions your organs and nerves—and without fat, you wouldn't be able to produce any hormones.

EAT HALF THE FAT— AND CHANGE THE TYPE

Obviously you can't subvert the laws of conservation of energy. Energy doesn't just disappear. Whatever you put into your body and don't burn off in your muscles makes a stopover in your fat cells. Consuming about 60 to 70 fat grams per day will keep you lean and fit, provided they don't all come from saturated animal fats. Animal fat should be kept to a minimum; it is not a fat burner. You're better off consuming unsaturated fatty acids. These are substances your body can't produce on its own. Good sources are vegetables, olives, nuts, seeds, and fish.

FATS THAT KEEP YOU THIN

Your kitchen should always contain olive oil, the traditional oil of the slender centenarians living on the Isle of Crete. Olive oil supplies fatty acids that adjust the settings of your hormone balance to Lean, Fit, and Healthy. The same can be said of the omega-3 fatty acids found in fish. They control your body's super-hormones, the eicosanoids. If you eat ocean fish (such as herring, salmon, or mackerel) at least twice a week, you will stimulate a good number of these types of eicosanoids that will in turn give you better health, more vitality, a lighter mood, and protection for your heart.

FAT AND HIGH-GLYCEMIC INDEX

If you eat your pasta with a cream sauce or your roast beef with mashed potatoes, the potatoes and pasta (both have a high-glycemic index) will increase the insulin in your blood, which will then immediately transport the fat in the beef or cream to your hips, and seal away the fat molecules inside the fat cells. This won't happen, however, if you eat your meat with whole-wheat pasta (low-glycemic index). In this case the insulin is kept at bay, and the fat from the meat can be burned off in the muscle cells. When planning you meals, remember the following:

✴ Avoid eating fatty foods with high-glycemic foods (steak with French fries, pasta with cream sauce, buttered bread with jam, pizza, chocolate croissants, white bread with cheese that is over 40% fat).

✴ Create fat-burning combinations: Lamb with whole-grain rice, turkey breast with boiled potatoes, chicken with vegetables, whole-wheat pasta with shrimp, mozzarella, or whole-wheat bread with tomatoes.

THE THIN COMMANDMENTS

✴ Use olive oil instead of animal fats. Use less butter, cream, and margarine.

✴ Practice "light" cooking: Brush oil onto non-stick pans for sautéing. Choose steaming and braising to preserve vitamins and your figure.

✴ Eat things with zero fat: Legumes, fruits, fresh fruits, and whole grains (rice, pasta, bread, muesli) contain little or no fat.

✴ Reduce your consumption of red meats and processed meats like sausage or bacon. Instead choose ocean fish, game, and poultry. Choose lean cuts of meat: Fillets, escalopes, and loins.

✴ Always purchase low-fat dairy products and avoid prepared products, even if they say "light." Nature always does it better.

Power from Protein
Make those pounds disappear as if by magic
and Vital Nutrients

Nature provides you with a miracle substance that takes off the pounds while you eat: Protein. Protein does this for two reasons:

1. Your body devotes a great deal of its energy to converting dietary protein to valuable body materials such as muscles, hormones, your immune system, materials for repairing cells, promoting youthfulness, and vitality. It does so by availing itself of stored fat. This makes protein a real fat burner.

2. Muscles and fat-burning hormones are made up of protein. If you don't consume 50 to 100 grams of this high-power fuel every day you will lose valuable muscle mass, become sluggish and consequently, gain weight. But don't look to red meats and processed meats as your protein source. These foods supply purines, artery-damaging cholesterol, and saturated animal fats. Healthy sources of protein are fish, poultry, legumes, and low-fat dairy products.

TOO LITTLE PROTEIN AND VITAL NUTRIENTS MAKE YOU FAT

Protein must be broken down in your stomach and intestines into its tiny building blocks, the amino acids. This is the only way this valuable material can be transported to the cells, fortify your immune system, and help build fat-burning hormones, muscles, nerves and organs. If vital nutrients aren't present, however, the protein remains in your intestines without doing its job. It doesn't serve as a fat burner or high-power fuel for your body. As a result, many people suffer from a lack of protein.

Obesity is your body's response to too many "dead" nutrients and not enough vital nutrients. Vitamins and minerals act as the agents of energy metabolism. If they aren't present, fat can't be broken down and protein can't be utilized, and converted to muscles and fat-burning hormones. In other words, you put on more and more weight.

THE SIX RULES OF SLIMNESS

1. Live naturally: Consume the fat burners available from nature. Every day eat five servings of fruits and vegetables. Snack on seeds and nuts, preferably raw. Reach for whole-grain and dairy products. Eat fish three to five times a week.

2. Get enough vitamin C: Ensure that you are getting enough vitamin C, which the body uses to break down fat. Citrus fruits are good sources or opt for a supplement.

3. Consider a nutritional supplement: Due to modern methods of food production, little that is healthy remains in our foods. Fill up your empty tank with high-quality vitamin and mineral supplement. Be conscious of the vital nutrients that burn fat: Calcium, magnesium, chromium, iodine, selenium, and B vitamins.

4. Eat fitness-promoting combinations: Always combine protein (dairy products, meat, and fish) with carbohydrates (vegetables, salad, and fruit). This will provide you with both the vitamins you need for protein metabolism and the sugar you need for your brain. It will force your body to use its cushion of fat, to convert the protein contained in foods into energy.

5. Stock up on protein: You need at least 0.4 grams of protein per pound of bodyweight. If you consume one serving of protein every four hours, you will always have enough materials to produce the fat-burning hormones STH (growth hormone) and norepinephrine.

6. Never skip a meal: If you don't have time to make a full meal, mix up a protein shake. Look for prepared mixes at a health food store. Instead of satisfying your hunger with an unhealthy sandwich, shake up a skinny drink and accompany it with fresh fruit.

LOW-FAT SOURCES OF PROTEIN

4 oz contains	g of fat	4 oz contains	g of fat
MILK & DAIRY PRODUCTS		**FISH**	
Buttermilk	0.5	Pike perch, sole, pollack	1
Cheddar	32	Salmon	14
Cottage cheese	2.9	Shrimp	1.4
Cream cheese, low-fat	0.3	Trout	3
Edam	28	Yellow perch	0.8
Feta	16		
Goat cheese	21	**MEAT AND POULTRY**	
Kefir	3.5	Chicken	2
Milk, low-fat	2	Corned beef	6
Mozzarella	16.1	Fillet of beef	4
Parmesan	25	Fillet of veal	1
Yogurt, low-fat	0.1	Ham	3
		Poultry sausage	5
FISH		Rabbit	3
Bismarck herring (filleted pickled herring)	16	Roast beef	5
Cod	0.8	Saddle of venison	4
Crayfish	1.1	Turkey breast	1
Flounder	2		
Lobster	1.9	**MISCELLANEOUS**	
Mackerel, smoked	16	Eggs	5.2
Mussels	1.3	Legumes, grains	Trace
Oysters	1.2	Tofu	5
Pike	0.9		

Power

Lose up to seven pounds in seven days with the glycemic index formula

Week

If you use the recipes in this book and follow the rules below, you can melt off a pound a day.

1. Exercise: Run or walk 30 minutes every morning on an empty stomach and at a moderate pace with a fat-burning pulse of around 130. Keep track with a pulse monitor. Breathe in for four steps and out for four steps, breathing deeply and regularly. And if the pulse monitor alarm goes off, slow down until you feel like speeding up again. Run once more in the evening.

2. Drink: Drink 3 quarts of water with fresh lemon juice every day. Drinking a 16-ounce glass of water after dessert and before leaving the table aids digestion. Avoid all drinks containing sugar as well as beer (high-glycemic index). A single glass of dry white wine is OK.

3. Eat: Eat fat-burning combinations regularly. If you need to skip a meal, shake up a protein drink instead and eat some fresh fruit.

4. Pre-eat: Before every meal, eat a large bowl of salad. Feel free to take a larger portion of whole-grain rice or pasta.

5. Train: Buy a latex exercise band with instructions. Exercise problem areas for 10 to 20 minutes, including your abdomen, hips, and buns. Your body will then form fat-burning muscles and hormones.

6. Avoid the scale: Measure your progress by the fit of your jeans rather than by the scale. You're in the process of reducing fat and building muscles, which are heavier than fat.

7: Avoid sweets: Snack on a bar of unsweetened chocolate, which has a low-glycemic index. A spoonful of fat burning Three Berry Jam will also do the trick (recipe on page 15). If you just can't stop thinking about chocolate, go running. The change of scene will redirect your thoughts.

AND AFTER THE FITNESS WEEK?

There is no "after." You will run and eat your way to a new, thin, active life. Use sugar like a spice, avoid white flour as much as possible. You don't have to practice total self-denial. It's a matter of what you do throughout the 365 days of the year. Just keep eating a lot of fat burners.

POWER WEEK

Monday

* Apple-Raspberry Muesli with Kefir * Tomato Stuffed with Radish Yogurt
* Zucchini Strips with Cured Salmon
* Spaghetti with Herb Pesto

Tuesday

* Whole-Wheat Rolls with Tomato * Strawberries with Two Dips
* Artichoke-Cherry Tomato Salad
* Monkfish Ragout with Lentils

Wednesday

* Berry-Pistachio Yogurt * Citrus-Spiked Fat Burner Drink
* Chicken Skewers with Cucumber-Radish Salad
* Oven Ratatouille with Millet

Thursday

* Radish-Cheese Spread on Pumpernickel * Raspberry-Mango Salad
* Marinated Asparagus with Turkey
* Sole with Spring Vegetables

Friday

* Bread with Three-Berry Jam * Tomato Bell Pepper Mix
* Seafood Cocktail with Broccoli
* Boiled Potatoes with Veggie-Garlic Dip

Saturday

* Avocado with Tomato Cottage Cheese * Blackberry Sherbet
* Kohlrabi and Mushroom Carpaccio
* Tuna Skewers with Saffron Rice

Sunday

* Tropical Fruits with Coconut-Lime Yogurt * Arugula Dip with Crispbread
* Tomato-Apple Salad with Arugula
* Bean Sprout and Chicken Stir-Fry

Berry-

Start your day with

Pistachio

fruit and protein

Yogurt

Serves 2: • 9 oz mixed berries or grapes • 2 tsp lemon juice • 1 tbs apple juice concentrate • 4 tsp pistachio nuts • 1 1/4 cups plain low-fat yogurt

Rinse the fruit briefly, drain and sort. Cut large fruit into smaller pieces. Toss the berries with the lemon juice and apple juice concentrate. Chop the pistachios and stir them into the yogurt. In small glass dishes, arrange alternating layers of berries and yogurt, saving 1/3 of the berries for sprinkling on top.

POWER PER SERVING: 151 CALORIES • 7 G PROTEIN • 5 G FAT • 21 G CARBOHYDRATES

Tropical Fruits with

The selenium in coconut makes you cheerful

Coconut-Lime Yogurt

Serves 2: • 1 papaya • 1 star fruit (whole foods market or Latin market) • 1 kiwi • 1 cup low-fat vanilla yogurt • 2 tbs unsweetened coconut milk • 2 tsp brown sugar • 1 tbs lime juice • 2 tsp grated coconut, toasted

Peel the papaya, remove the seeds and slice. Wash and slice the star fruit. Peel the kiwi and cut it into wedges. Arrange the fruit decoratively on a plate. Mix the yogurt with the coconut milk, sugar, and lime juice. Drizzle the coconut mixture over the fruit or serve it in a bowl alongside. Garnish with the grated coconut.

POWER PER SERVING: 170 CALORIES • 14 G PROTEIN • 2 G FAT • 23 G CARBOHYDRATES

Apple-Raspberry Muesli

A real brain food combination

with Kefir

Serves 2: • 2 tbs pumpkin seeds • 4 tbs rolled oats • 1 tbs raisins • 1 apple • 1 tbs lemon juice • 4 oz fresh raspberries • 1 1/2 cups kefir (natural foods store) • 2 tsp maple syrup

Toast the pumpkin seeds, and mix them with the oats and raisins. Divide the mixture among two small bowls. Peel the apple and grate it, avoiding the core. Toss the grated apple with the lemon juice. Briefly rinse the raspberries, removing any foreign matter. Mix the kefir and maple syrup. Sprinkle the apples and raspberries over the oat mixture, and pour the kefir over the top.

POWER PER SERVING: 280 CALORIES • 12 G PROTEIN • 10 G FAT • 34 G CARBOHYDRATES

Bread with
Fat burner jam to feed your sweet tooth
Three-Berry Jam

Rinse the berries briefly, sort and trim them, and cut into small pieces. In a saucepan, simmer the berries, fructose, and ascorbic acid for 5 minutes over low heat.

Stir the agar-agar into the cold water, add it to the saucepan, and simmer for an additional 2 to 3 minutes over low heat.

Immediately transfer the berry jam to two small glass canning jars with screw tops, seal them tightly, and let cool. Tip: Sterilize the jars first by boiling the jars and the lids in water for 5 minutes; fill them while still hot.

To eat, spread 1 tbs of the cream cheese and 2 tbs of the jam on each slice of bread. Garnish with mint. Store the remaining jam in the refrigerator and consume as quickly as possible.

Serves 2:

9 oz mixed ripe berries

2 1/2 oz fructose (natural foods store)

1 tsp granulated ascorbic acid (natural foods store)

1/2 tsp agar-agar (vegetable gelling agent— natural foods store)

2 tbs cold water

2 tbs low-fat cream cheese

2 slices whole-wheat bread

1 sprig fresh mint

Whole-Wheat Bread

White bread has a high-glycemic index and is a true fat storer. On the other hand, most whole-grain breads are fat burners. Whenever possible, spread your whole-wheat bread with low-fat cream cheese as an accompaniment to jam instead of butter. Whole-wheat bread is also an excellent accompaniment to vegetables and salad.

POWER PER SERVING:

240 CALORIES

5 G PROTEIN • 2 G FAT

52 G CARBOHYDRATES

Whole-Wheat Rolls

The secret to eternal youth from Crete

with Tomato

Thoroughly mash the herb paté with a fork and mix it with the tomato paste, lemon juice, and olive oil until smooth. Season to taste with pepper and salt.

Serves 2:
1/4 cup vegetarian herb paté (natural foods store)
3 tsp tomato paste (preferably organic)
1 tsp lemon juice
1 tsp olive oil
Black pepper to taste
Salt to taste
2 whole-wheat rolls
2 tomatoes
2 sprigs fresh basil

Slice the rolls in half horizontally, and spread the paté mixture on all of the halves, dividing evenly. Wash the tomatoes, remove the cores and cut them into small wedges.

Arrange the tomato wedges on the roll halves. Sprinkle with a little salt and pepper. Wash the basil, shake it dry, pull off the leaves and use them to garnish the rolls.

Tomatoes

Tomatoes raise your spirits, are tonic for your heart and liver, and help prevent gout and rheumatism. They contain the antioxidant lycopene, which helps prevent cancer. Tomatoes also contain minerals that stimulate fat burning, including magnesium, calcium, iron, and zinc. They also contain potassium, which is a natural diuretic.

POWER PER SERVING:

196 CALORIES

8 G PROTEIN • 5 G FAT

30 G CARBOHYDRATES

Radish-Cheese Spread

Spicy slices of vital nutrients

on Pumpernickel

Serves 2: • 1 tsp butter, softened • 1/2 tsp brown mustard • 2 large slices pumpernickel bread
• 2 oz radishes • 2 oz Camembert cheese • Black pepper to taste • 1 tbs radish sprouts

Mix the butter and mustard, and spread it on the pumpernickel slices. Wash and trim
the radishes. Cut the radishes and Camembert into thin slices. Arrange the radishes and
Camem-bert in an overlapping pattern on the bread slices. Season with freshly ground
pepper and sprinkle with the radish sprouts.

POWER PER SERVING: 152 CALORIES • 10 G PROTEIN • 6 G FAT • 15 G CARBOHYDRATES

Smoked Salmon with

Fish—a superior fat burner

Horseradish and Apple

Serves 2: • 2 tbs low-fat cream cheese • 1 tsp grated fresh horseradish • Black pepper to taste
• 1/4 medium apple • 2 tsp lemon juice • 2 slices dark rye bread • 2 sprigs fresh dill • 2 oz smoked salmon

Mix the cream cheese with the horseradish and a little pepper. Wash the apple, cut it into thin
slices, and immediately drizzle it with the lemon juice. Spread the horseradish mixture on the
bread slices and cut them in half diagonally. Wash the dill and shake it dry. Arrange the apple
slices, smoked salmon, and dill sprigs on the bread, dividing evenly.

POWER PER SERVING: 158 CALORIES • 10 G PROTEIN • 6 G FAT • 15 G CARBOHYDRATES

Avocado with

A recipe for beauty, a slender figure, and healthy nerves

Tomato Cottage Cheese

Wash and quarter the tomato, remove the seeds and core, and cut it into small cubes. Cut the avocado in half and remove the pit. Scoop out the avocado flesh from the peel with a large spoon, leaving only a thin outer layer inside the peel halves and dice the flesh. Immediately drizzle the lemon juice over the avocado halves and diced avocado. Mix the cottage cheese with the diced tomato and diced avocado. Season with a little salt and pepper. Transfer the mixture to the hollowed-out avocado halves, sprinkle with the chopped chives, and serve.

Serves 2:

1 tomato

1 ripe avocado

2 tsp fresh lemon juice

1/2 cup cottage cheese

Salt to taste

Black pepper to taste

1 tbs chopped fresh chives

Avocados

Although this green exotic is the fattiest of fruits, it is loaded with unsaturated fatty acids that are essential to a healthy diet. They promote soft skin, healthy cell walls and strong nerves, and program your body's hormones to burn fat. Eat avocados and the fat storing hormone, insulin doesn't stand a chance.

POWER PER SERVING:

394 CALORIES

10 G PROTEIN • 38 G FAT

2 G CARBOHYDRATES

Raw Vegetables with
Dip into vitality
Herbed Cream Cheese

Mix together the cream cheese, mineral water, lemon juice, salt and pepper, and stir until smooth. Peel and mince the garlic. Wash the parsley, shake it dry, and set several leaves aside. Finely chop the remaining parsley leaves. Stir the chopped parsley and garlic into the cream cheese mixture.

Trim and wash the radishes. Trim and wash the celery and cut it into slices. Cut the bell pepper in half and remove the stem, ribs, and seeds, then wash it and cut it into strips. Cut the bread into little triangles. Decoratively arrange the radishes, celery, and pepper strips around the dip. Garnish with the remaining parsley leaves and serve with the bread triangles.

Serves 2:
4 oz low-fat cream cheese
2 tbs mineral water
2 tsp lemon juice
Salt to taste
Black pepper to taste
1 clove garlic
1/4 bunch fresh Italian parsley
4 oz radishes
2 stalks celery
1 small yellow bell pepper
1 slice whole rye bread

POWER PER SERVING: 122 CALORIES • 11 G PROTEIN • 1 G FAT • 16 G CARBOHYDRATES

Arugula Dip
Triggers a flood of "happiness hormones"

with Crispbread

Serves 2: • 3 oz arugula • 2 tbs pumpkin seeds • 2 tbs freshly grated Parmesan cheese

• 2 tsp balsamic vinegar • 2 tbs olive oil • 4–5 tbs vegetable stock • Salt to taste • Balck pepper to taste

• 1 green onion • 2 slices rye crispbread

Trim, sort, wash, and chop the arugula. Place the arugula, pumpkin seeds, Parmesan, vinegar, and olive oil in a blender or food processor, and process to a smooth purée. Stir in the stock to form a creamy paste, and season with salt and pepper. Wash and trim the green onion, slice it into fine rings, and add it to the paste. Break up the crispbread and use it for dipping.

POWER PER SERVING: 262 CALORIES • 9 G PROTEIN • 22 G FAT • 11 G CARBOHYDRATES

Bell Pepper
Fat-burning enzymes do their part

Pineapple Salsa

Serves 2: • 10 oz pineapple • 1/2 red bell pepper • 1/2 small red onion • 1 tbs lime juice • Salt to taste

• Tabasco sauce to taste • 2 tsp olive oil • 1 tbs chopped fresh cilantro • Whole-wheat toast

Peel the pineapple and cut it into small cubes, avoiding the tough core. Wash and trim the bell pepper, and dice it finely. Peel the onion and chop it finely. Stir together the pineapple, bell pepper, onion, lime juice, salt, Tabasco, olive oil, and cilantro. Serve with the whole-wheat toast.

POWER PER SERVING: 95 CALORIES • 1 G PROTEIN • 5 G FAT • 12 G CARBOHYDRATES

Tomato Stuffed with Radish Yogurt

Essential oils keep you fit

Serves 2: • 2 large, ripe tomatoes • 4 oz radishes • 3/4 cup plain nonfat yogurt •

• 2 tbs chopped fresh chives • Salt to taste • Black pepper to taste • 1 tsp lemon juice

Wash the tomatoes. Slice off the top of each tomato and scoop out the tomato flesh with a spoon (save the flesh for another use, if desired). Wash and grate the radishes. Mix the grated radishes with the yogurt and 1 tbs of the chives. Season the mixture with salt, pepper, and lemon juice. Fill the tomatoes with the radish yogurt and sprinkle with the remaining chives.

POWER PER SERVING: 64 CALORIES • 5 G PROTEIN • 1 G FAT • 9 G CARBOHYDRATES

Zucchini Rounds with Mushrooms

A deposit in your health account

Serves 2: • 3 oz white mushrooms • 1 green onion • 2 tsp fresh lemon juice • 1 tsp balsamic vinegar

• 1 1/2 tbs olive oil • Salt to taste • Black pepper to taste • 8 oz large zucchini

Trim, wash, and slice the mushrooms and green onion. Mix them with the lemon juice, vinegar, 1 tbs of the olive oil, salt, and pepper. Trim and wash the zucchini, cut it into 8 slices and season with salt. Brush the remaining oil in a skillet and heat to medium. Sauté the zucchini slices for a few minutes on both sides, and season with salt and pepper. Place the zucchini on serving plates and top with the mushrooms.

POWER PER SERVING: 87 CALORIES • 3 G PROTEIN • 7 G FAT • 3 G CARBOHYDRATES

Ham-Wrapped

These slender stalks are true fat burners

Asparagus with Basil Dip

Serves 2:
10 oz asparagus
Salt to taste
1 tsp olive oil
1/2 cup plain low-fat yogurt
2 tbs sour cream
1 tsp small capers (drained)
1 tsp fresh lemon juice
Black pepper to taste
12 fresh basil leaves
2 oz lean smoked ham

Wash the asparagus, break off the woody ends, and peel the bottom third of the stalks. In a saucepan, bring a generous amount of salted water to a boil with the oil. Add the asparagus, cover, reduce the heat, and simmer until tender-crisp, about 10 to 12 minutes.

For the dip, mix the yogurt and sour cream. Finely chop the capers and mix them in. Season the dip with lemon juice, salt, and pepper. Wash and shake dry the basil leaves and set several leaves aside. Chop the remaining leaves finely and mix them into the dip. Drain the asparagus, plunge it into ice water to stop the cooking, and drain again.

Wrap the ham around the asparagus and arrange on a platter. Garnish the dip with the remaining basil.

Lighten Up Your Sauces

One-half cup of cream contains 31 fat grams and the same amount of crème fraîche contains 40 grams. Instead of using these ingredients, try lightening up your sauces. Try, for example, puréed vegetables, which have a delicate taste and a smooth texture. Or you can replace the cream with low-fat buttermilk, sour cream, or yogurt.

POWER PER SERVING:

185 CALORIES

9 G PROTEIN • 14 G FAT

6 G CARBOHYDRATES

Cucumber-Shrimp

The best fat burners come from the sea

Salad

Serves 2:
1/4 cup frozen peas
2 tsp sunflower kernels
Salt to taste
7 oz cucumber
4 oz peeled cooked shrimp
2 red leaf lettuce leaves
1/4 bunch fresh dill
1/2 cup kefir (natural foods store)
1 tsp fresh lemon juice
1 tsp canola oil
Black pepper to taste
Pumpernickel crackers

Thaw the peas. In an ungreased skillet, toast the sunflower kernels until golden brown. Peel, dice, and lightly salt the cucumber. Rinse the shrimp and drain. Wash the lettuce, shake it dry, and tear it into bite-sized pieces. Wash the dill, shake it dry, and set aside 2–3 sprigs. Remove the leaves from the remaining sprigs and chop. In a large bowl, stir together the kefir, lemon juice, and canola oil until smooth. Season with salt and pepper. Add the peas, cucumber, shrimp, lettuce, and dill to the bowl and toss well. Divide the salad among serving plates, sprinkle with sunflower seeds, garnish with the remaining dill, and serve with pumpernickel crackers.

Shrimps for Taurine

Shrimp provides taurine, a protein substance that helps the pituitary gland to send out its fat melting hormones, such as the growth hormone that builds up muscles and breaks down fat. This valuable fat burner can also be found in mussels, poultry, and liver.

POWER PER SERVING:

166 CALORIES

14 G PROTEIN • 6 G FAT

14 G CARBOHYDRATES

power

Raspberry-Mango Salad

Snack yourself to slenderness

Serves 2: • 1 ripe mango • 6 oz fresh raspberries • 1/2 cup low-fat cottage cheese • 1/2 cup plain low-fat yogurt • 1 tsp honey • 2 tsp pine nuts, toasted • 1 sprig fresh mint

Peel the mango, cut thin wedges away from the pit, and arrange them on a serving dish. Rinse the raspberries briefly, sort them, and sprinkle them over the mango wedges. Stir together the cottage cheese, yogurt, and honey and pour over the top. Sprinkle with pine nuts. Wash the mint, remove the leaves from the stem, and use them to garnish the salad.

POWER PER SERVING: 199 CALORIES • 6 G PROTEIN • 7 G FAT • 23 G CARBOHYDRATES

Blackberry Sherbert

A craving for ice cream? Go right ahead!

Serves 2: • 9 oz fresh blackberries • 2 tsp lemon juice • 1 tbs maple syrup • 1/4 cup water • 1 sprig fresh mint

Wash and drain the blackberries. Set a few berries aside and purée the rest together with the lemon juice, maple syrup, and water. Place the blackberry purée in a stainless steel bowl, cover, and freeze 3–4 hours, stirring at 1-hour intervals. Transfer the sherbet to dessert bowls, and garnish with the remaining berries and mint.

POWER PER SERVING: 82 CALORIES • 2 G PROTEIN • 1 G FAT • 14 G CARBOHYDRATES

Strawberries
Fruit for your sweet tooth
with Two Dips

Rinse, sort, and drain the strawberries.

For the chocolate dip, chop the chocolate coarsely.
Place it in a bowl with 3 tbs of the milk. In a double
boiler, that is hot but not boiling, melt the chocolate
over low heat while stirring constantly. Let the
chocolate dip cool.

For the vanilla dip, slit open the vanilla bean
lengthwise, scrape out the seeds with a small knife,
and mix them with the honey, the remaining 1 tbs
milk, and the yogurt.

Arrange the strawberries decoratively on a plate,
and serve them with the chocolate and vanilla dips.

Serves 2:
9 oz fresh strawberries
1 1/2 oz unsweetened chocolate
1/4 cup low-fat milk
1/2 vanilla bean
1 tsp floral honey
1/4 cup low-fat vanilla yogurt

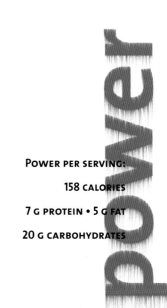

POWER PER SERVING:

158 CALORIES

7 G PROTEIN • 5 G FAT

20 G CARBOHYDRATES

Kiwi-Strawberry

A sweet fat burner cocktail

Shake with Mint

Serves 2 drinks: • 1 kiwi • 3–4 oz fresh strawberries • 2 tsp chopped fresh mint • Juice from 1 lime • 2 tsp maple syrup • 2 tbs quick-cooking oatmeal • 1/2 cup plain low-fat yogurt • 1/2 cup cold milk

Peel and dice the kiwi. Wash and trim the strawberries and cut them into small pieces. Put the mint, lime juice, maple syrup, oat flakes, and yogurt in a blender and purée for about 15 seconds. Add the milk and purée vigorously once again. Pour into two large glasses and serve with wide straws.

POWER PER DRINK: 83 CALORIES • 2 G PROTEIN • 1 G FAT • 17 G CARBOHYDRATES

Tomato

A spicy fat burner cocktail

Bell Pepper Mix

Serves 2 drinks: • 3 oz red bell pepper • 3 oz celery root (celeriac) • 2 tbs chopped fresh Italian parsley • 1/2 tsp red chile flakes • 1 1/4 cups cold tomato juice • Salt to taste • Black pepper to taste • 4 ice cubes

Trim and wash the bell pepper, peel the celery root, and dice both vegetables. Put the pepper, celery root, parsley, chile flakes, and 1/2 cup of the tomato juice in a blender and purée. Add the remaining juice and purée vigorously. Season with salt and pepper. Fill 2 glasses with ice cubes, pour the mixture over the top, and serve with wide straws.

POWER PER DRINK: 50 CALORIES • 3 G PROTEIN • 1 G FAT • 8 G CARBOHYDRATES

Citrus-Spiked
The slimming power of tropical fruits
Fat Burner Drink

Plunge the tomatoes into boiling water for a few seconds, transfer them to ice water, drain, and pull off the tomato skins. Cut the tomatoes in half and squeeze out the seeds. Chop the tomatoes coarsely. Trim the carrot, peel, and grate it finely. Remove the seeds from the papaya half, peel, and dice it. Put the tomatoes, carrot, and papaya in a blender. Squeeze the juice from the oranges and lemon, and add to the blender. Add the fructose, ascorbic acid, and olive oil. Blend for 15 seconds at high speed.

Pour the drink into 2 tall glasses. Slit the lemon slices and place on the rim of each glass. Serve with wide straws.

Serves 2 drinks:

2 ripe tomatoes
1 medium carrot
1/2 ripe papaya
2 oranges
1 lemon
1 tsp fructose
(natural foods store)
Dash of ascorbic acid granules
(natural foods store)
1 tsp olive oil
2 slices lemon

Tropical Fruits for Enzymes

Papaya, pineapple, and mango provide enzymes that indirectly boost fat burning. These enzymes break down protein and help transport valuable fat burners to your cells where they do their job of promoting your health and fitness.

POWER PER DRINK:

153 CALORIES

4 G PROTEIN • 3 G FAT

32 G CARBOHYDRATES

Artichoke-Cherry
Essential fatty acids trigger fat-burning hormones
Tomato Salad

Add the lemon juice to a medium bowl of water. Break the stems off the artichokes.

Cut off the top third of the artichoke leaves. Pull out the inner leaves and the

inedible fuzzy center to expose the heart. Trim the hearts and

immediately place them in the lemon water.

For the salad dressing, whisk together the vinegar, herb salt,

and pepper. With a whisk, gradually beat in the olive oil, canola

oil, and sunflower oil.

Drain the artichoke hearts, cut them into very thin strips, and

mix them with the dressing.

Meanwhile, peel the shallot and garlic, and chop both finely.

Wash the cherry tomatoes, cut larger ones in half, and remove

the stems. Add the shallot, garlic, tomatoes, capers, and parsley

to the bowl with the artichokes and mix well. Season the salad

generously with salt and pepper.

Serves 2:
Juice of 1/2 lemon
2 small artichokes (about 18 oz)
1 1/2 tbs white wine vinegar
Herb salt to taste
Black pepper to taste
2 tbs olive oil
1 tsp canola oil
1 tsp sunflower oil
1 shallot
1 clove garlic
8 oz cherry tomatoes
1 tsp capers (drained)
2 tbs chopped fresh Italian parsley

POWER PER SERVING: 217 CALORIES • 3 G PROTEIN • 18 G FAT • 13 G CARBOHYDRATES

Kohlrabi and
Raw food for nutrition and energy
Mushroom Carpaccio

Serves 2: • 1 tbs sesame seeds • 10 oz kohlrabi • 2 oz mushrooms • 1 green onion • 1 tbs white wine vinegar • Salt to taste • Black pepper to taste • 2 tbs sunflower oil • 1/2 tsp sesame oil • Whole-wheat bread

In a dry nonstick skillet, toast the sesame seeds. Peel the kohlrabi, cut it into quarters, slice it thinly, and arrange on 2 plates. Clean the mushrooms and cut them into very thin cross sections. Trim the green onion and wash and cut it into rings. Distribute the mushrooms and onion over the kohlrabi. Whisk together the vinegar, salt, pepper, sunflower oil and sesame oil, and drizzle it over the top. Sprinkle with the toasted sesame seeds. Serve with whole-wheat bread.

POWER PER SERVING: 150 CALORIES • 5 G PROTEIN • 12 G FAT • 7 G CARBOHYDRATES

Tomato-Apple Salad
With fat-burning fruits and vegetables
with Arugula

Serves 2: • 4 ripe tomatoes • 1/2 tart apple • 1 carrot • 1 1/2 oz arugula • 1 tbs lemon juice

• 1 tsp balsamic vinegar • Salt to taste • Black pepper to taste • 2 tbs olive oil

• 1 1/2 oz Parmesan cheese • Whole-wheat bread

Wash the tomatoes and cut them into 8 wedges. Cut the apple in half, remove the core, and cut into slices. Peel and grate the carrot. Rinse the arugula, shake dry, remove the stems, and chop. Whisk together lemon juice, vinegar, salt, pepper, and oil. Toss the tomatoes, apple, grated carrot, and arugula with the dressing. With a vegetable peeler, shave the Parmesan over the top. Serve with whole-wheat bread.

POWER PER SERVING: 221 CALORIES • 8 G PROTEIN • 18 G FAT • 8 G CARBOHYDRATES

Tex-Mex Salad

With the fat-burning factor methionine

with Kidney Beans

Rinse and drain the beans. Cut the bell pepper in half and remove the stem, ribs and seeds, and wash and cut it into strips. Cut the avocado in half, then remove the pit and peel. Cut the avocado halves into narrow wedges and immediately drizzle them with the lemon juice. Wash and trim the celery and cut it diagonally into thin slices. Peel the onion, cut it in half, then cut it into half-rings.

Make the dressing: Whisk together the vinegar, salt, pepper, Tabasco, and oil in a medium bowl. Wash the parsley and cilantro, shake it dry, chop it, and add to the dressing. Stir the vegetables into the dressing. Wash the lettuce, shake it dry, and arrange on serving plates. Spoon the vegetables on top of the lettuce leaves.

Serves 2:

4 oz canned red kidney beans (drained)
1 yellow bell pepper
1 avocado
1 tsp lemon juice
1 stalk celery
1 small red onion
2 tbs red wine vinegar
Salt to taste
Pepper to taste
Tabasco sauce to taste
3 tbs extra-virgin olive oil
1/4 bunch fresh cilantro or Italian parsley
4 iceberg lettuce leaves

Legumes for Methionine

Methionine is an important substance for building up protein. A deficiency weakens your immune system, increases your risk for cancer, and causes you to put on weight. Without methionine, there would be no formation of carnitine, which transports fat from your hips to be combusted in your muscles. Good sources of methionine include legumes, fish, poultry, and cheese.

POWER PER SERVING:

377 CALORIES

5 G PROTEIN • 35 G FAT

12 G CARBOHYDRATES

Curried Veal Fillet
with Tomato Yogurt

A hearty way to lose weight

Serves 2:
1 medium tomato
1 small red onion
1 cup plain low-fat yogurt
5 sprigs fresh Italian parsley
Salt to taste
Black pepper to taste
1/2 tsp ground coriander
2 tsp lemon juice
2 cups vegetable stock
7 oz boneless veal
1 tsp curry powder
Dark rye bread

Wash the tomato, cut it in half, squeeze out the seeds, and dice the flesh finely. Peel the onion and dice it finely. Mix together the tomatoes, onion, and yogurt. Wash the parsley, shake it dry, chop it finely, and mix half of it into the tomato yogurt. Season with salt, pepper, coriander, and lemon juice; cover and refrigerate.

In a deep-sided skillet, bring the vegetable stock to a boil. Cut the veal into thin slices. Rub each veal piece with a little curry powder and place in the skillet. Reduce the heat to low and simmer the veal for about 5 minutes. Remove the meat, and season with salt and pepper. Sprinkle with the remaining parsley. Serve the veal with the tomato yogurt and dark rye bread.

Sour Helpers

Vinegar and lemon juice are true slenderizers. Eating a salad with vinegar before a meal of fish, or sprinkling lemon juice over a chicken breast or turkey escalope helps your stomach break down protein and helps your body metabolize it better, thus speeding it to its final destination—the 70 billion cells in your body—where it can do its slenderizing work.

POWER PER SERVING

213 CALORIES

27 G PROTEIN • 5 G FAT

13 G CARBOHYDRATES

Marinated Asparagus

Asparagus reduces weight and blood pressure

with Turkey

Serves 2:

18 oz asparagus

Salt to taste

1 egg

2 tsp pine nuts

2 tbs lemon juice

1 tbs white wine vinegar

Black pepper to taste

2 tbs extra-virgin olive oil

4 oz cherry tomatoes

8 fresh basil leaves

2 oz sliced smoked turkey breast

Wash the asparagus, break off the woody ends, and peel just the lower third of the stalks. Bring a pot of salted water to a boil. Add the asparagus, reduce the heat, and simmer until tender-crisp, about 10–12 minutes. Boil the egg for 10 minutes, until it is cooked hard, then plunge it into cold water. In an ungreased skillet, toast the pine nuts until golden brown. Drain the asparagus, setting aside 3 tbs of the asparagus water. For the marinade, whisk together the lemon juice, vinegar, salt, pepper, oil, and reserved asparagus water. Pour the marinade over the asparagus in a shallow dish and refrigerate for 2–3 hours. Peel the egg and cut it into 8 wedges. Wash the tomatoes and cut them in half. Wash and shake dry the basil, and chop the leaves coarsely. Arrange the egg wedges, tomatoes, and turkey breast alongside the asparagus on serving plates. Sprinkle with the pine nuts and basil.

Skinny Sticks

From April to June you can let yourself go and fill up with asparagus. These skinny sticks contain only 15 calories per 4 oz. The asparagine in asparagus stimulates your kidneys, acting as a natural diuretic. Other fat-burning factors in asparagus are fiber, vitamin C, iron, calcium, and iodine.

POWER PER SERVING

260 CALORIES

15 G PROTEIN • 19 G FAT

9 G CARBOHYDRATES

Chicken Skewers with

Poultry + lemon = a perfect fat-burning combination

Cucumber-Radish Salad

Serves 2: • 8 oz boneless, skinless chicken breast • 2 tbs lemon juice • Salt to taste • Black pepper to taste • 2 tbs olive oil • 9 oz cucumber • 9 oz radishes • 1 tsp red chile flakes • 2 tbs chopped fresh Italian parsley

Cut the chicken breast into cubes and thread them onto 2 wooden skewers. In a shallow dish, mix together 1 tbs of the lemon juice, salt, pepper, and 1/2 tbs of the oil. Add the chicken skewers and turn to coat them well with the marinade. Peel the cucumber. Trim and wash the radishes. Cut the cucumber and radishes into slices. Mix together the remaining 1 1/2 tbs lemon juice, 1 1/2 tbs oil, salt, pepper, and the chile flakes. Add the cucumber, radishes and parsley, and toss well. Broil the skewers in the oven for 8–10 minutes. Serve the chicken with the salad.

POWER PER SERVING: 283 CALORIES • 26 G PROTEIN • 16 G FAT • 6 G CARBOHYDRATES

Zucchini Strips

Loaded with omega-3 fatty acids

with Cured Salmon

Serves 2: • 10 oz zucchini • 2 tbs olive oil • Salt to taste • Black pepper to taste • 2 tsp balsamic vinegar • 4 oz sliced cured salmon (gravlax) • 2 tbs plain low-fat yogurt • 2 slices dark whole-grain bread

Wash and trim the zucchini, then cut it lengthwise into thin slices. Brush a nonstick skillet with some of the oil, add the zucchini slices a few at a time, and sauté for 2–3 minutes on both sides over medium heat. Transfer the zucchini to a shallow bowl, sprinkle with salt, pepper, vinegar and the remaining oil, and marinate for 2 hours. Serve with the salmon, yogurt, and bread.

POWER PER SERVING: 300 CALORIES • 17 G PROTEIN • 24 G FAT • 4 G CARBOHYDRATES

Seafood Cocktail
An extra-light feast
with Broccoli

Cut the cod into strips and the squid into pieces. Rinse the mussels, pull off any hairy filaments, and discard any that are open. In a saucepan, bring 1/2 cup water to a boil. Simmer the fish strips and squid in the water for 2–3 minutes over low heat; remove them from the water and set aside. Place the mussels in the cooking liquid, cover the pot, and simmer until the shells open, about 3–5 minutes. Remove the mussels from the stock and pull the mussel meat from the shells. Discard any unopened mussels.

Trim the broccoli and blanch it for 3 minutes in boiling, salted water. Plunge the broccoli into cold water and drain. Trim the bell pepper, wash it, and cut it into strips. Trim the green onion, wash it, and cut into rings.

In a medium bowl, whisk together the soy sauce, lemon juice, sugar, salt, and pepper. Stir the cilantro, cod strips, squid, mussels, and vegetables into the marinade. Serve with the baguette.

Serves 2:

4 oz cod fillet

4 oz squid rings or tentacles (cleaned)

10 oz fresh mussels (in the shell)

10 oz broccoli

Salt to taste

1 small red bell pepper

1 green onion

2 tbs soy sauce

2 tbs lemon juice

1 tsp brown sugar

Black pepper to taste

1 tbs chopped fresh cilantro or Italian parsley

Whole-wheat baguette

 Seafood: The Super Fat Burner

The protein in seafood stimulates fat burning. Seafood provides you with an abundance of tyrosine, an amino acid that your body uses to produce the fat-burning hormones norepinephrine and dopamine. Seafood also provides iodine, the fuel for an active thyroid.

POWER PER SERVING:

159 CALORIES

25 G PROTEIN • 2 G FAT

10 G CARBOHYDRATES

Spaghetti with Herb Pesto

Laced with three herbs

Plunge the tomatoes into boiling water for a few seconds, transfer them to ice water, drain, and pull off the tomato skins. Cut the tomatoes into quarters, remove the seeds, and cut them into small cubes. In a saucepan, bring a generous amount of salted water to a boil, and cook the spaghetti according to the package instructions, until it is al dente. For the pesto, rinse the chervil, parsley, and basil, shake dry, remove the leaves from the stems, and chop them coarsely. Peel and chop the garlic. Put the chervil, parsley, basil, garlic, vinegar almonds, and Parmesan in a blender or food processor. Add 4–6 tbs water from the spaghetti and process into a fine purée. Gradually drizzle in the oil, and season to taste with salt and pepper.

Serves 2:
18 oz tomatoes
Salt to taste
5 oz whole-wheat spaghetti
Handful of fresh chervil
1/4 bunch fresh Italian parsley
6 large fresh basil leaves
1 small clove garlic
2 tsp balsamic vinegar
2 tbs chopped almonds
1 oz Parmesan cheese, grated
2 tbs olive oil
Black pepper to taste

Drain the pasta, put into a warmed serving bowl, and immediately add the diced tomato, salt, and pepper. Add the pesto to taste, toss well, and serve.

Herbs

Herbs magically transform dishes, maintain your health, calm and relax you, stimulate you and keep you thin. Mixing herbs in recipes gives you maximum nutritional benefit. For example, in the pesto above, chervil promotes circulation and aids digestion; parsley activates your metabolism; and basil fortifies and soothes your stomach.

POWER PER SERVING:

434 CALORIES

17 G PROTEIN • 4 G FAT

41 G CARBOHYDRATES

Boiled Potatoes with

High-glycemic and low-fat

Veggie-Garlic Dip

Scrub the potatoes and boil them in salted water until tender, about 20–25 minutes. Remove the stem, ribs and seeds from the bell pepper, and wash and cut it into cubes. Peel the cucumber and dice it finely. Trim the green onions, wash, and cut it into fine rings. Peel the garlic and chop it finely. Mix together the cream cheese, milk and lemon juice, and season generously with salt and paprika. Add the diced bell pepper and cucumber, garlic and two-thirds of the green onion. Wash and shake dry the dill, chop all but a few sprigs, and stir it into the cream cheese mixture. Garnish the cream cheese mixture with the remaining green onions and dill. Drain the potatoes, wait until they're cool enough to handle, peel them, and serve with the dip.

Serves 2:
1 lb small potatoes
Salt to taste
1/2 red bell pepper
4 oz cucumber
2 green onions
1 small clove garlic
8 oz low-fat cream cheese
3 tbs low-fat milk
2 tsp lemon juice
1/2 tsp hot Hungarian paprika
1/4 bunch fresh dill

Potatoes

Potatoes have a high-glycemic index. Combine them with fat and the insulin weight gain is complete. That's why we suggest you use a lighter version: 100 grams of boiled potatoes have 0.3 grams of fat, French fries fatten your figure with 14.6 fat grams and chips complete the job with 40 grams of fat. To combat their fat-storing potential, eat potatoes with low-fat cream cheese, lean fish, poultry, or vegetables.

POWER PER SERVING:

243 CALORIES

23 G PROTEIN • 1 G FAT

35 G CARBOHYDRATES

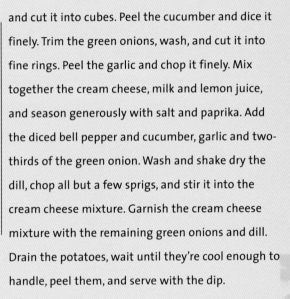

Oven Ratatouille

Pamper your body with lots of vegetables

with Millet

Preheat the oven to 450°F. Cut the bell peppers into quarters. Remove the stems, ribs and seeds, and wash and cut them into pieces. Wash and trim the zucchini and eggplant. Cut the zucchini into slices and the eggplant into large cubes. Peel the onion and dice it coarsely. Wash the tomatoes, cut them into quarters, remove the seeds, and cut them into pieces. Peel and chop the garlic.

Grease a casserole with 1 tbs of the oil and heat in the oven for 5 minutes. Put the vegetables in the casserole and season with salt, pepper and the herbes de Provence. Drizzle the vegetables with the remaining 1 tbs oil and the lemon juice. In the meantime, bring 1/2 cup of the stock to a boil and pour it over the vegetables. Bake the vegetables on the middle oven rack for 30 minutes, stirring occasionally.

Serves 2:

1 small red bell pepper

1 small green bell pepper

4 oz zucchini

4 oz eggplant

1/2 medium onion

8 oz Roma tomatoes

2 cloves garlic

2 tbs olive oil

Salt to taste

Black pepper to taste

1 tsp herbes de Provence

1 tbs lemon juice

3/4 cup vegetable stock

2/3 cup millet

2 tbs chopped fresh Italian parsley

Bring the remaining stock to a boil, add the millet, and cook for 25 minutes over low heat, until the millet is tender. Stir in the parsley and season with salt and pepper. Serve the cooked millet with the ratatouille.

POWER PER SERVING: 464 CALORIES • 11 G PROTEIN • 19 G FAT • 61 G CARBOHYDRATES

Gazpacho with

Carotenoids in tomatoes and bell peppers keep you fit

Croutons

Serves 2:
2 slices stale whole-wheat bread
Salt to taste
7 oz tomato
1 small red bell pepper
1 small green bell pepper
4 oz cucumber
1 clove garlic
1 tsp tomato paste
(preferably organic)
1 cup cold tomato juice
3 tbs vegetable stock
2 tsp olive oil
1–2 tsp lemon juice
1 tsp brown sugar
Cayenne pepper to taste

Cut 1 bread slice into cubes, sprinkle with salt, and soak in 1/4 tbs lukewarm water. In the meantime, plunge the tomato into boiling water for a few seconds, transfer it to ice water, drain, and pull off the tomato skins. Cut the tomatoes in half, squeeze out the seeds, and chop the flesh coarsely. Remove the stems, ribs and seeds from the bell peppers, and wash and dice them. Peel the cucumber, cut it in half lengthwise, scrape out the seeds with a spoon and dice. Peel and chop the garlic.

In a blender or food processor, put the soaked bread, tomatoes, garlic, half each of the red pepper, green pepper, and cucumber, the tomato paste, tomato juice, and stock. Add 1 tsp of the olive oil, the lemon juice, sugar, salt, and cayenne pepper. Process until the mixture is smooth. Cover and refrigerate for 1 hour.

Cut the remaining bread slice into small cubes. In a skillet, heat the remaining 1 tbs olive oil over medium heat. Add the bread cubes and sauté until golden brown. Stir the puréed mixture, pour it into 2 soup bowls, and sprinkle with the remaining diced vegetables and the croutons.

POWER PER SERVING: 166 CALORIES • 5 G PROTEIN • 6 G FAT • 22 G CARBOHYDRATES

Risotto with

Stay slim with whole-grain rice

Raw Vegetables

In a dry skillet, toast the pumpkin seeds and let them cool. Heat the stock in a small saucepan until boiling, then keep warm. Peel the onion and garlic and dice finely. In a saucepan, heat the oil over medium heat and sauté the onion and garlic in it until translucent. Add the rice, toast it briefly, while stirring constantly, and season with salt. Add the wine and simmer until it has nearly evaporated. Add about 1/2 cup of the hot vegetable stock to the rice. Cook the rice for 35–40 minutes, stirring occasionally and gradually adding more stock. The rice is done when it is tender, but still has a slight firmness at the center when you bite into a grain.

While the rice is cooking, wash and trim the zucchini. Peel the carrot. Grate both vegetables. When the rice is done, stir the grated vegetables into it, season with salt and pepper, cover, and let stand for 5 minutes. Sprinkle the risotto with the pumpkin seeds and cheese.

Serves 2:
1 tbs pumpkin seeds
1 2/3 cups vegetable stock
1 onion
1 small clove garlic
1 tbs olive oil
1/2 cup short-grain brown rice
(natural foods store)
Salt to taste
1/4 cup dry white wine
4 oz zucchini
4 oz carrot
Black pepper to taste
1 1/2 oz Swiss cheese, grated

Whole-Grain Rice

Fiber, such as found in whole-grain rice, rescues you from insulin weight gain. Enzymes in your intestines break down the starch of rice or grain into sugar molecules. The fiber from the grain hulls keeps the enzymes from doing this too quickly. As a result, sugar enters your bloodstream more slowly and triggers only a little of the fat storing hormone insulin.

POWER PER SERVING:

484 CALORIES

12 G PROTEIN • 18 G FAT

65 G CARBOHYDRATES

Green Garbanzo

Legumes provide lots of fat-burning protein

Bean Stir-Fry

Wash the spinach well, remove the stems, and chop it coarsely. Cut the bell pepper into quarters, remove the stem, ribs and seeds, and wash and cut it into strips. Trim the green onions, wash, and cut it diagonally into pieces. Wash and trim the peas, removing any strings. Peel the ginger and garlic, and chop them finely. In a wok or skillet, heat the oil over high heat and briefly sauté the ginger and garlic in it. Add the pepper strips, peas and green onions, and sauté for about 4 minutes, stirring constantly. Add the spinach, garbanzo beans and stock, and stir-fry for an additional 2–3 minutes. Season to taste with salt, cayenne pepper, and lemon juice. Transfer the mixture to plates and place 1 tbs yogurt in the center of each serving.

Serves 2:

8 oz spinach leaves

1 green bell pepper

5 oz green onions

4 oz sugar snap peas

1 small piece fresh ginger

1 clove garlic

1 tbs canola oil

9 oz cooked garbanzo beans (drained)

3 tbs vegetable stock

Salt to taste

Cayenne pepper to taste

1–2 tsp lemon juice

2 tbs plain low-fat yogurt

Guaranteed Vitamins

Select vegetables that are in season and come from your own region. Always adhere to these basic principles: Buy fresh, use as soon as possible, don't cut up into pieces that are too small, don't soak too long, and cook gently. Follow the traffic light rule: One red, one green, and one yellow vegetable every day. This will guarantee a wide variety of vitamins and phytochemicals in your diet.

POWER PER SERVING:

492 CALORIES

42 G PROTEIN • 13 G FAT

82 G CARBOHYDRATES

Instant

Enjoy light pizza

Veggie Pizza

For the dough, quickly knead together the yogurt, flour, baking powder, milk, 2 tbs of the oil, and 1/2 tsp salt. Preheat the oven to 400°F. Line a baking sheet with parchment paper. On a lightly floured work surface, roll out the dough to a thin rectangle and transfer it to the baking sheet. Pierce the dough several times with a fork. Distribute the tomatoes over the dough. Clean the mushrooms and cut into very thin slices. Trim the fennel, wash, cut it into quarters, and then into thin slices. Distribute the mushrooms and fennel over the tomatoes. Season the pizza with salt, and sprinkle with the red pepper flakes and cheese. Drizzle the remaining 1/2 tbs oil over the top. Bake the pizza for 25–30 minutes on the middle oven shelf. Garnish with olives and basil, and serve.

Serves 2:

1/2 cup plain low-fat yogurt
1 cup all-purpose flour
1 tsp baking powder
3 tbs low-fat milk
2 1/2 tbs sunflower oil
Salt to taste
5 oz canned tomato pieces (drained)
3 oz mushrooms
1 small bulb fennel
1 tsp red pepper flakes
2 oz Gouda cheese, grated
6 black olives (pitted)
6–8 fresh basil leaves

Chiles Spice up Your Figure

Eat something spicy and your brain will be flooded with endorphins, the messenger chemicals that ease pain and lift your spirits. A good mood translates into a more active and slender you. Spiciness also heats up the fat cells, causing them to be more likely to move.

POWER PER SERVING:

545 CALORIES

23 G PROTEIN • 23 G FAT

64 G CARBOHYDRATES

Bean Sprouts and
Wok cooking preserves nutrients
Chicken Stir-Fry

Cut the chicken breast into thin strips and season with pepper. Rinse and drain the bean sprouts. Remove the stem, ribs and seeds from the bell pepper, and wash and cut it into strips. Trim the celery, wash, and cut it into thin slices. Peel the onion and dice it finely. In a small bowl, whisk together the chicken stock, soy sauce, sherry, and cornstarch in a bowl.

In a wok or skillet, heat 1 tbs of the oil over high heat. Stir-fry the chicken for about 3 minutes, then remove it from the pan. In the remaining oil, stir-fry the bell pepper, celery, and onion for 3 minutes. Add the sprouts and stir-fry for 1 minute.

Stir in the soy sauce mixture and stir-fry until the sauce thickens, about 2 minutes. Add the chicken, briefly heat through, and season with pepper. Sprinkle with cilantro and serve over the rice.

Serves 2:

7 oz boneless, skinless chicken breast

Black pepper to taste

7 oz bean sprouts

1 bell pepper

2 stalks celery

1 small onion

1/2 cup chicken stock

2 tbs soy sauce

2 tbs dry sherry

1 tsp cornstarch

1 1/2 tbs soybean oil

2 tbs chopped fresh cilantro

Cooked brown rice

POWER PER SERVING: 315 CALORIES • 37 G PROTEIN • 8 G FAT • 19 G CARBOHYDRATES

Spinach

A lighter version of a beloved classic

Saltimbocca

Wash the spinach well and remove the stems. Blanch the spinach in boiling, salted water for 1 minute, plunge it into cold water and drain. Squeeze the moisture out of the spinach and chop it coarsely. Season with salt, pepper, and nutmeg.

Place 1 tbs of the spinach on top of each chicken medallion, fold them over, and fasten each one with a toothpick or wooden skewer. In a skillet, heat the oil over medium-high heat. Sauté the chicken medallions in the oil for 1–2 minutes on each side, remove them from the pan, and season with salt and pepper and keep warm. Mix together the lime juice, wine, stock and cornstarch, and add it to the skillet. Simmer over low heat until the mixture thickens. Season the sauce with salt and pepper. Add the chicken and the remaining spinach to the skillet and simmer, covered, for 2–3 minutes. Serve with the pasta.

Serves 2:
10 oz fresh spinach
Salt to taste
Black pepper to taste
Freshly grated nutmeg to taste
4 thin chicken medallions
(about 2 oz each)
1 tbs olive oil
Juice of 1 lime
1/4 cup dry white wine
1/2 cup chicken stock
2 tsp cornstarch
Cooked whole-wheat fettuccine

White Meat

Meat is an important source of protein and iron, which makes it a fat burner. At the same time, however, beef, lamb, and pork contain a large amount of fat and purines. You should keep your consumption of red meat to a minimum. When you do indulge, choose the lower fat pieces from the fillet or tenderloin. Best of all, use white meat. Poultry and veal help you to go easy on bad fat.

POWER PER SERVING:

325 CALORIES

30 G PROTEIN • 14 G FAT

17 G CARBOHYDRATES

Sole with
Rich in iodine
Spring Vegetables

Season the sole fillets with salt and pepper, and spread each with 1/2 tbs of the crème fraîche. Wash and shake the tarragon dry, then remove the leaves from the stems. Sprinkle some of the tarragon leaves over the sole fillets and roll them up tightly. Peel the kohlrabi and cut it into quarters. Peel the carrots. Cut both vegetables into thin slices. Trim and wash the sugar snap peas. Peel and dice the onion.

In a saucepan, heat the oil over medium heat. Add the onion and sauté until translucent. Add the kohlrabi, carrots and peas, and briefly sauté. Pour in the stock, cover the pan, and simmer the vegetables for 5 minutes. Season the vegetables with salt and pepper. Stir in the remaining crème fraîche. Place the rolled sole on top of the vegetables, cover, and simmer for 10 minutes over low heat. Chop the remaining tarragon and sprinkle on top. Serve with the rice

Serves 2:
4 sole fillets (about 2 oz each)
Salt to taste
White pepper to taste
1 1/2 tbs crème fraîche
1 sprig fresh tarragon
1 kohlrabi
7 oz baby carrots
5 oz sugar snap peas
1 small onion
1 tbs canola oil
2/3 cup vegetable stock
Cooked brown and wild rice

Fish, Please!

You should eat fish at least twice a week. It makes no difference what type—all fish is healthy. Salmon provides omega-3 fatty acids that prevent many chronic illnesses. Mackerel contains tyrosine, the material of fat-burning hormones. Fillet of sole is virtually fat-free.

POWER PER SERVING:

276 CALORIES

37 G PROTEIN • 13 G FAT

42 G CARBOHYDRATES

Stir-Fried Vegetables

Melt away fat with fish protein

with Shrimp

Serves 2:

5 oz sugar snap peas
Salt to taste
1 yellow bell pepper
1 shallot
1 tbs canola oil
Pepper to taste
5 oz raw peeled shrimp
4 oz cherry tomatoes
1/4 bunch fresh dill
1 tbs fresh lemon juice

Trim and wash the sugar snap peas. Blanch the peas in boiling, salted water for 1 minute, plunge them into cold water, and drain. Remove the stem, ribs and seeds from the bell pepper, and wash and cut it into strips. Peel the shallot and finely chop. In a skillet, heat the oil over medium heat. Add the peas, bell pepper and shallot, and sauté for 5 minutes. Season with salt and pepper.

Add the shrimp and sauté over low heat for 2 minutes. Cut the tomatoes in half and remove the stems. Wash the dill, shake dry, and chop. Add the tomato halves and dill to the skillet, and cook for an additional 2 minutes. Remove from the heat and toss with the lemon juice.

Midnight Snacks

Just before going to bed, raid the refrigerator one last time. For efficient fat burning you'll need protein and carbohydrates. Half a serving of yogurt with 2 tbs of oat flakes stimulates the hormone serotonin for a peaceful sleep as well as growth hormone, which breaks down fat and builds up muscle while you quietly slumber.

POWER PER SERVING:

161 CALORIES

33 G PROTEIN • 5 G FAT

43 G CARBOHYDRATES

Monkfish Ragout

Fill up your tank with "super"

with Lentils

Wash and peel the potatoes and carrot, then dice them. Trim the leek, slit it open lengthwise, and wash and cut it into rings. Peel and dice the onion.

Serves 2:
5 oz firm potatoes
1 carrot
1 small leek
1 small onion
2 tsp olive oil
1 cup vegetable stock
7 oz cooked brown lentils
1/2 cup organic tomato sauce
Salt to taste
Black pepper to taste
10 oz monkfish fillet
2 tsp lemon juice
2 tbs chopped fresh Italian parsley

In a wide saucepan, heat the oil over medium heat and sauté the onion in it until translucent. Add the potatoes, carrot and leek, and sauté for 3 minutes. Pour in the stock, cover, and simmer for 10 minutes over low heat.

Add the lentils, tomato sauce, salt, and pepper. Simmer the mixture for an additional 3 minutes over medium heat.

Cut the fish into cubes, and season it with the lemon juice, salt, and pepper. Add the fish to the pan, cover, and simmer for 3–4 minutes over low heat. Season to taste with salt and pepper. Sprinkle parsley over the top.

58

Olive Oil

Olive oil is the fountain of youth in Mediterranean countries. You too can cook with this precious tonic for a healthy heart and a slender figure. And don't skimp on the quality. Go for the purest and most natural "extra virgin" oil.

POWER PER SERVING:

565 CALORIES

49 G PROTEIN • 9 G FAT

70 G CARBOHYDRATES

Tuna Skewers
Feast and stay thin
with Saffron Rice

Peel the onion and dice it finely. In a saucepan, heat 1 tbs of the oil over medium heat and briefly sauté the onion in it. Add the saffron and the rice, and sauté for 2 minutes. Pour in the wine and let it simmer. Heat the stock, stir it into the rice, cover the pan, and cook for 40 minutes over low heat.

Cut the tuna into 1/2 inch cubes. Peel the onion and cut it into eighths. Remove the stem, ribs and seeds from the pepper, and wash and cut it into pieces. Wash and trim the zucchini and cut into thick slices. Rinse and shake dry the sage. Alternately thread pieces of fish, onion, bell pepper, zucchini, and sage onto wooden skewers. Peel and mince the garlic, and mix it with the lemon juice, salt, and pepper in a shallow dish. Add the tuna skewers to the dish, coat the ingredients with the marinade, and set aside for about 30 minutes.

In a skillet, heat the remaining 1 tbs oil over medium heat. Sauté the skewers for 12–15 minutes, turning occasionally. Season the saffron rice with salt and pepper, and serve with the tuna skewers.

Serves 2:
1 small red onion
2 tbs olive oil
2 pinches powdered saffron
3/4 cup short-grain brown rice
1/4 cup dry white wine
1 1/4 cups vegetable stock
5 oz tuna fillet
1 small white onion
1 small yellow bell pepper
4 oz zucchini
8 fresh sage leaves
1 small clove garlic
1 tbs lemon juice
Salt to taste
Black pepper to taste

POWER PER SERVING: 570 CALORIES • 18 G PROTEIN • 25 G FAT • 63 G CARBOHYDRATES

Index

Abbreviations

tsp = teaspoon
tbs = tablespoon

Credits

Published originally under the
title Fatburner Rezepte: Mit der er-
folgreichen GLYX-Formel bis
zu 7 Pfund in 7 Tagen weniger

© 2000 Gräfe und Unzer Verlag
GmbH, Munich
English translation copyright for
the US edition: ©2001 Silverback
Books, Inc.

Project editor: Lisa M. Tooker
Editor and reader: Maryna Zim-
dars, Jennifer Newens, CCP
Cover design: Independent
Medien-Design, Claudia Fillmann
Inside layout: Heinz Kraxenberger
Production: Helmut Giersberg,
Patty Holden
Photos: FoodPhotography
Eising, Munich
ISBN: 1-930603-26-6
Printed in China

Caution
The techniques and recipes in this
book are to be used at the reader's
sole discretion and risk. Always
consult a doctor before beginning
a new eating plan.

Marion Grillparzer has a degree
in food science and is a trained
journalist. She lives in Munich
and works as a freelance journalist;
she has written for a number of
magazines for many years. She is
the author of numerous books fo-
cusing on nutrition and health

Martina Kittler first studied food
science and sports before turning
her passion for cooking into a ca-
reer. For almost eight years she
worked as an editor for one of the
largest German cooking magazines.
Since 1991, she has been writing
books and magazine articles as a
freelance author. Her main subjects
are modern, healthy nutrition and
quick-and-easy everyday recipes.

Susie M. and **Pete Eising** have
studios in Munich, Germany, and
Kennebunkport, Maine. They both
studied at the Professional Academy
for Photodesign in Munich where,
in 1991, they opened their own
food photography studio.

For this book:
Photographic design:
Martina Görlach
Food styling:
Monika Schuster

SILVERBACK

BOOKS, INC.